Copyright © 2024 Jessica Hottle

All rights reserved, including the right to reproduce this book or portions of this book in any form whatsoever without the prior written permission of the copyright holder.

Scripture quotations marked esv are taken from the ESV® Bible (The Holy Bible, English Standard Version®), copyright © 2001 by Crossway, a publishing ministry of Good News Publishers. Used by permission. All rights reserved.

Scripture quotations marked tlb are taken from The Living Bible copyright© 1971. Used by permission of Tyndale House Publishers, Inc., Carol Stream, Illinois 60188. All rights reserved.

Limits of Liability and Disclaimer of Warranty
The author and publisher shall not be liable for your misuse of this material. This book is strictly for informational and educational purposes.

The purpose of this book is to educate and entertain. The author and/or publisher does not guarantee that anyone following these techniques, suggestions, tips, ideas, or strategies will become successful. The author and/or publisher shall have neither liability nor responsibility to anyone with respect to any loss or damage caused, or alleged to be caused, directly or indirectly by the information contained in this book.

Cover design and layout by Allison Capps.

Anger

BIBLICAL STUDY

Jessica Hottle

Introduction

Anger is an emotion that hits hard, has some of the most intense reactions, and can be felt deeply in the body. It doesn't matter if you are someone who feels their feelings, shoves down their feelings, or has difficulty communicating them; anger will be an emotion often felt. Anger can be one of your defense mechanisms or one of your greatest strengths (in terms of righteous anger).

Throughout this study, you will see practical, biblical, and clinical explanations of anger. I want you to see how anger affects the whole body, not just how you may feel for the day. I pray that through this study, you will better understand what God says about anger and how to manage it better when it arises. Anger is unavoidable because we are humans living in a fallen world. That is not an excuse for anger but a fact. Anger is one of the most basic emotions we, as humans, feel and experience.

I aim to help you befriend the feeling of anger instead of running from it. Remember: Feeling anger is not a sin. What you do with and in your anger can lead you to sin. I carried anger around with me for most of my life. It became my defense mechanism so people wouldn't get too close and to keep the pain I deeply felt behind a wall. Through God's grace in my life, I have been able to walk through forgiveness and recognize that when anger comes, it results from hurt, and God is right there with me to see me through it.

Maybe you got this biblical study on anger because you are tired, overwhelmed, and worn out trying to do this all on your own. You desire community but are afraid of being hurt again, or you know this anger you feel is starting to affect other areas of your life, and you want help and healing from it. No matter the "why," God is here with you and ready to walk with you every step of the way.

What is Anger

Anger can be the fruit of many roots. Anger arises within us when we don't live up to an expectation we place on ourselves. We also experience anger when something painful or wrong happens to us or those around us. Anger can fill our hearts when someone mistreats or does something to cause harm. Anger might arise from a wounded ego, in response to injustice in the world, or as a byproduct of emotional pain. Anger, when used maturely, can also be a response to evil.

Here are also some fundamental beliefs that can trigger anger within us:

- We believe we must always do well. If we don't mess up, don't get it right, or are not perfect in something, we get angry, which can also start a cycle of self-hatred.

- We believe everyone must treat us well. When someone doesn't treat us well, we get angry. Not saying this is right or wrong. But when we place high expectations on others to be perfect, we will become angry when they fail because they are human.
- We believe following God should feel good (or be more accessible than this). We get angry at God when life doesn't feel good. We spend a lot of time reconciling a "not-so-good experience" with a "good God." "If God is good, then why all the bad," we think to ourselves. When it doesn't feel good, we get angry.

Whenever life bumps up against one of these beliefs, anger comes. Anger is an emotional response to a real or perceived wrongdoing or threat. It can also be one of the chief emotions that sabotages our minds and way of viewing others around us.

We can identify anger anywhere from mild irritation to explosive rage: hidden, repressed, or openly expressed. When our bodies experience anger, they go through this process:

1. Our adrenaline increases.
2. Our bodies release sugar.
3. Our hearts beat faster.
4. Our blood pressure increases.

5. Our pupils enlarge.
6. Our fists clench while our jaw tightens.
7. Our ability to remain alert increases.

Think about this for a moment. The body still responds this way when we remain angry, even when we are unaware of it at the moment. We might forget we are angry, but our bodies do not forget. They are constantly telling the story about what we feel.

As we move forward in this study, I will discuss the two types of anger we see in scripture: righteous and fleshly. Righteous anger grieves over sin and evil, while fleshly anger allows the devil to take a foothold in our lives and causes us to sink further into the sinful lusts of the flesh. Fleshly anger is the leading cause of misery, depression, sickness, and loss (which is the one we will focus on working through in this study).

Righteous Anger

"Righteous anger" in the Bible refers to a type of justified and moral anger. This type is often associated with God's anger, provoked by injustice, sin, and disobedience. In this context, God's wrath is righteous because of its aim: correcting wrongs and restoring justice and righteousness. This anger is neither petty nor selfish but instead is purposeful, always aimed at reinforcing moral order and good.

The Bible acknowledges righteous anger but also cautions that it's challenging for human anger to be genuinely righteous because of our inherent fallibility and sinfulness. The expectation is to strive to respond with patience, understanding, and love, even when confronting injustice or wrongdoing, which James encourages us of in James 1:19-20, *"Know this, my beloved brothers: let every person be quick to hear, slow to speak, slow to anger; for the anger of man does not produce the righteousness of God."*

One example people often refer to with righteous anger is when Jesus flipped the tables. We read about this in Matthew 21:12-13, *"And Jesus entered the temple and drove out all who sold and bought in the temple, and he overturned the tables of the money-changers and the seats of those who sold pigeons. He said to them, "It is written, 'My house shall be called a house of prayer,' but you make it a den of robbers."*

The context of this scripture is Jesus had cast the money changers out of the temple nearly three years earlier at the start of His ministry (See John 2:14-17). However, they went back to their practices of selling animals and cheating the people. So, I'm sure part of what Jesus noticed was their return to the practices He had so violently reproved nearly three years before. Yet He didn't take action that day. His second temple cleansing occurred the day after this record of Him noticing what was happening in the temple (See Mark 11:12 and 15-17). The anger expressed when He drove the money changers out the second time was premeditated, yet it wasn't a sin (See Hebrews 4:15 and 7:26).

Jesus dealt with sin without sinning. We often deal with sin by sinning because we take what happened to us into our own hands, or we think we need to be the ones who make something right that was actually wrong. We must know our heart's motives when dealing with and handling the sin around us.

Therefore, how do we know if we are operating in righteous anger? Here are three ways we can identify if our anger is righteous or if we are acting out of our flesh:

Righteous anger reacts against actual sin. Godly anger is provoked by sin as defined or described in the Bible. There is an Old Testament example of righteous anger in the Bible, specifically in the life of the prophet Elijah. In 1 Kings 18, we see Elijah confronting the people of Israel and the prophets of Baal on Mount Carmel. Elijah steps forward, filled with righteous anger and love for the Lord. Before calling on God, he repairs the altar of the Lord that had been broken. Then, he prays a concise yet powerful prayer. In response to Elijah's prayer, God sends fire from heaven, consuming the sacrifice, the wood, the stones, and even the water in the trench around the altar. Righteous anger is not an opportunity to use our personal wishes as the standard for what is right and wrong.

Righteous anger is God-oriented, not me-oriented. "He must increase, but I must decrease," were the words spoken by Jesus's cousin, John the Baptist (John 3:30). Godly anger focuses not on how my reputation and purposes have been slighted but on how God's reputation and purposes have been offended. We want our character and heart to align with God's concerns. Romans 8:29 reminds us of who we are becoming, *"For those whom he foreknew he also predestined to be conformed to the image of his Son, in order that he might be the firstborn among many brothers."*

Righteous anger expresses itself in godly ways. Anger directed at actual sin and that is God-oriented must also have the characteristics of the fruit of the Spirit (Gal 5:22-23) if it is to be called righteous. For example, it must have love as its aim, be patient, and have self-control. Ultimately, when operating in righteous anger, the action will be in response to sin, any action will be God-oriented, and both actions and words should point to the truth and bear the fruit of the Spirit out of love for God and toward others.

Fleshly Anger

Fleshly anger keeps us in bondage and thinking that our way of doing things is the best way. We want to take matters into our own hands and correct what was wrong. It's destructive, aggressive, and often carries a lot of unforgiveness. Fleshly anger gives birth to resentment, which can give birth to bitterness.

For reference, let's look at Matthew 5:21-23, *"You have heard that it was said to those of old, 'You shall not murder; and whoever murders will be liable to judgment.' But I say to you that everyone who is angry with his brother will be liable to judgment; whoever insults his brother will be liable to the council; and whoever says, 'You fool!' will be liable to the hell of fire."*

Through this passage, we can see there is a fine line between anger and sin. Jesus is not saying never to get angry; He doesn't command us not to get angry. It would be impossible not ever to be angry. Instead, we have to be able to differentiate between anger as an emotion versus the behavioral response to anger. Aggression describes the behavioral reaction of anger (rage).

Let's take a closer look at Matthew 5:21-23 for a better understanding by examining a few keywords and phrases. The first phrase, "whoever is angry," means to "brood over and repay the offense over" like a grudge you carry around. That's the word Jesus uses here. Therefore, what He is saying by "whoever is being angry and remaining angry" or "nursing a grudge" in her heart at a brother or sister is that person will be subject to judgment as a murderer.

The second word we must examine is "racca;" which would be considered an insult or "to consider another one stupid." Using this term would be an offense worthy of answering to the court, which was the Jewish council at Jerusalem made up of priests, scribes, and elders. Furthermore, the definition of "fool" in this passage is calling someone immoral and unintelligent, which is where we get the modern word moron. Throughout this passage, we read how Jesus carefully described the progression from hurling an insult like "stupid" or "idiot" to judging the whole person. It's a significant shift from shaming their behavior to shaming their character itself.

Moving on to verse 23, Jesus says they will be in danger of the "fire of hell." The fire of hell referred to a real place in Jesus' time, a place people would have known and been familiar with in their locale. There was a valley outside of Jerusalem, the valley of Gehenna. It was a place where children were slaughtered in worship of other gods. This valley was somewhere no one wanted to end up.

The valley of Gehenna was a garbage dump that became a picture of hell over time: a place of burning sewage, flesh, and garbage. Maggots and worms crawled through the waste, and the smoke smelled strong and sickening (Isaiah 30:33). It was utterly filthy, disgusting, and repulsive to the nose and eyes.

Gehenna presented such a vivid image that Christ used it to symbolize hell: a place of eternal torment and constant uncleanness, where the fires never ceased burning, and the worms never stopped crawling (Matthew 10:28; Mark 9:47-48). This reference in scripture was not only a legitimate place of idol worship but also could be in reference as a metaphor for the judgment to come.

What can we take from studying this passage? There is a difference between addressing the problem the person caused versus condemning the person for the problem. In our anger, we insult and call people fools. According to scripture, both of these have consequences, which are the "fire of hell" and answering to the court. The main point is, before death, what is happening to us right now when anger is all-consuming? This anger puts us at odds with a brother or sister in Christ and creates a wedge between us and God. I've learned it isn't what happened to me that torments me the most. What distresses me the most is the anger I hold onto and the forgiveness I refuse to give.

We may think, "I know it's not good to call people an idiot," but is it genuinely subject to the fire of hell? Is it that big of a deal? Jesus presents us with a picture of "hell on earth," telling us murder comes from the same birthplace in the heart where an insult comes alive. When we carry a heart posture of anger, let's remember what James 1:20 says, *"For the [resentful, deep-seated] anger of man does not produce the righteousness of God [that standard of behavior which He requires from us]."*[1] (AMP) Therefore, the anger we carry that we think is justified and will bring justice through our strength is a false illusion and a snare the enemy uses to keep us from experiencing the true justice only Christ can give.

Therefore, the Bible warns us about letting anger rule the heart. When we let anger take over, it can lead to saying hurtful things or judging others. Jesus tells us it's not just about being angry but about holding onto that anger, nursing grudges, and insulting people. He uses strong words, talking about being in danger of hell, using a place called Gehenna as an example. He uses the valley of Gehenna to paint a picture of the consequences of unchecked anger. The point is, it's not just about drastic events like murder; even insulting someone has its consequences. Next time you experience anger, remember not to allow that feeling to take over your heart and mind. Instead, attempt handling your emotions in a way that aligns with how God wants you to live—showing love and understanding to others.

---

[1] Amplified Bible. (2015). The Lockman Foundation. https://www.biblegateway.com/passage/?search=james+1%3A20&version=AMP

Three Responses to Anger

There are usually three ways we respond to anger. We repress, suppress, or express our anger. Let's look at what each of these means and what they look like in our everyday lives.

When we repress our anger, we act in a state of denial. It can even be scary or uncomfortable to allow ourselves to express how we feel or acknowledge our anger. However, when we repress our anger, we tend to have (and experience) heightened bodily expressions of anger, such as high blood pressure. Repressing anger is like sweeping dirt under a rug. At first, it might appear tidy and controlled, but over time, the hidden emotions accumulate and create a messy, unaddressed situation. Just as the dirt doesn't disappear, repressed anger can linger beneath the surface, affecting our emotional well-being and potentially surfacing unexpectedly in unrelated situations.

Suppressing our anger is when we acknowledge the feeling of anger but don't express it. Someone suppressing anger may try to keep everything in without talking about it or addressing the anger they are experiencing. We can become emotionally critical, impatient, and demanding. Suppressed anger often results in outbursts where we let it build inside until one day, and we can't take it anymore. It's like trying to hold a beach ball underwater. At first, it might seem manageable, but the more you try to contain it, the greater the pressure builds up. Eventually, if you're not careful, it can burst out unexpectedly, causing a splash that affects you and those around you. Like the beach ball, emotions, especially anger, need a healthy outlet for expression. They need direction and release rather than holding them back with force.

Lastly, whenever we express our anger, this will often result in control and manipulation. We can also express anger verbally (shouting, cursing, arguing, or yelling) or physically (throwing things, breaking objects, hitting walls, or getting into fights). Expressing anger is like a boiling kettle. When the pressure builds up, it needs a release valve, and if we don't let off steam in a controlled way, the lid might blow off. Similarly, expressing anger in a healthy manner allows for releasing pent-up emotions and prevents the situation from reaching a boiling point where it becomes uncontrollable and potentially harmful.

Handling our anger with compassion is essential for our well-being and aligns with the idea of seeking God's healing. Ignoring or suppressing anger creates a burden that can weigh heavily on our hearts and minds. We invite God's healing into our lives by compassionately approaching our emotional struggles. Recognizing and understanding our anger, expressing it in healthy ways, and fostering positive connections with others are not only acts of self-care but also opportunities for divine healing. In navigating our emotions with love and understanding, we open ourselves to God's grace, allowing Him to restore our hearts and harmony in our relationships.

The Seven Stages of Anger

While there are three ways we respond to anger, there are seven stages we go through when we are angry. These stages serve as a guide, offering insight into the unfolding of our anger—from its initial stirrings to its eventual resolution or expression. Understanding these seven stages provides us the tools to navigate our emotions with kindness and self-awareness, encouraging us to embrace healthier approaches to expressing and managing this intense emotion. By acknowledging and understanding these stages, we can cultivate compassion for ourselves and others, fostering a deeper understanding of the complexities that come with the human experience of anger. Most importantly, Ephesians 4:26 reminds us that when our anger is left unchecked, it can become a foothold for the enemy in our lives, *"Go ahead and be angry. You do well to be angry—but don't use your anger as fuel for revenge. And don't stay angry. Don't go to bed angry. Don't give the Devil that kind of foothold in your life."*[2]

2   The Message: The Bible in Contemporary Language. (2002). Eugene Peterson, https://www.biblegateway.com/passage/?search=ephesians+4%3A26-27&version=MSG

Let's seek to understand the stages of anger so we can move through them as good stewards of our emotions.

Seven Stages of Anger:
1. Triggered
2. Wounded Ego
3. Victim
4. Contempt
5. Verbal Expression
6. Harm to Others
7. Abuse

The first stage is that something is triggered, and we get angry. Sometimes consciously but often time subconsciously. Something inside or outside of ourselves annoys us, makes us unhappy, or hurts us. We get angry in many ways, but the first stage is becoming triggered.

The second stage is the wounded ego: when we experience an injured ego or pride from anger. This stage is where we take it as an insult to our identity. We believe the offender is insulting who we are as a person. We may think, "How could they do this to me?"

The third stage of our anger is when we become a self-righteous victim. Whenever we are in a situation with someone else, and they hurt us, we condition ourselves to be an innocent victim while everyone else is the problem.

The fourth stage is when we shift from being a self-righteous victim to giving our heart over to contempt. We start to think more of ourselves (that we are better) than the person who wronged us. We feel good about ourselves because we believe we would never do that. We write off not just their behavior but their character. In this stage, we highlight their weakness while we highlight our strengths.

In this fifth stage, we express it after processing everything internally. Our oral comments can begin to surface, and stewing thoughts become spoken words.

In the sixth stage, we can experience "hell on earth" because our anger has gone unchecked. Our anger may have shifted to rage and is harming other people.

In this seventh stage, if we allow our anger to grow to this stage, we start to abuse others in various capacities.

What may start as a disagreement may gradually become contempt for the other person, and we begin to write them off because our way must be the right way (and the only way). Anger becomes dangerous when we give in to it and allow it to rule our hearts.

We see two fundamental principles in the Kingdom of God. First, that righteousness is an inward matter of the heart and not only an external work. And second, that the quality of our fellowship with God is conditional upon our heart posture towards other people. Our relationship with God is woven throughout our relationships with people. Referring back to Matthew 5:21-23 (these verses together with the verses preceding them), we see that righteousness (harmony) applies to our external obedience to the commandments (do not murder) and to our internal obedience (do not be angry.) We also see that how we treat others affects our present fellowship with others, as well as with God and our future Kingdom prospects on the Day of Judgment.

Working through the seven stages of anger with God is a journey marked by understanding and kindness. Feeling mixed emotions is normal when things don't go as planned. During these times, we can turn to the Scriptures, like Psalm 34:18, which reminds us, " The Lord is near to the brokenhearted and saves the crushed in spirit." Talking to God about our anger helps us move through these stages with His guidance. In prayer, we can ask for wisdom and strength, remembering Proverbs 3:5-6, which encourages us to *"Trust in the Lord with all your heart, and do not lean on your own understanding. In all your ways acknowledge him, and he will make straight your paths."* This process is a compassionate way to invite God into our struggles, letting His grace guide us toward healing and understanding for ourselves and those around us.

Consequences of Anger

When people think of the book of Jonah, I think they often think of Jonah's disobedience to God. God told Jonah to go to Nineveh, but Jonah decided to go in the other direction, ignoring God's command completely.

Now the word of the Lord came to Jonah the son of Amittai, saying, "Arise, go to Nineveh, that great city, and call out against it, for their evil has come up before me." But Jonah rose to flee to Tarshish from the presence of the Lord. (Jonah 1:1-3)

However, if we look a little deeper at Jonah's disobedience, we understand why he decided to go the other way and try to flee from the presence of the Lord. During Jonah's time as a prophet, and during his time, the Assyrians became great in power. They were a particular threat to the nation of Israel. Jonah, going to prophesy to Nineveh, would send him into his enemy's territory. As you continue to read through the book of Jonah, it appears that Jonah didn't want the people of Nineveh to repent (hence his reluctance to go to Nineveh and call out their evil). Why didn't he want Nineveh to repent?

Nineveh was Assyria's capital and Israel's enemy; therefore, it wasn't Jonah's desire to see his enemies prospering and blessed. He wanted them all to die. Since Assyria was becoming great in power, they were threatening to invade the nation of Israel, where Jonah lived. Jonah knew if Nineveh and the Assyrian empire were destroyed, it would benefit his people. We could sum up his reluctance to preach repentance to the people of Nineveh, as Jonah wanted Nineveh destroyed so that his nation could survive.

Jonah knew that if the Ninevites repented, the Lord would turn away from the judgment He intended, and that's the reason Jonah didn't want to preach in Nineveh. He had told the Lord this when the Lord first told him to preach in Nineveh. Understanding that this is why Jonah was mad gives excellent insight into the actions of the Lord in this chapter. The Lord taught Jonah a lesson in the proper value of people.

And he prayed to the Lord and said, "O Lord, is not this what I said when I was yet in my country? That is why I made haste to flee to Tarshish; for I knew that you are a gracious God and merciful, slow to anger and abounding in steadfast love, and relenting from disaster. (Jonah 4:2)

How does this apply to anger? We may wish our enemies destruction, but God loves all men and "does not will that any should perish" (2 Peter 3:9). This shows God's value for all people, His Imago Dei. The Lord taught Jonah a lesson in the proper value of people. The book of Jonah can show us where anger can take us: disobedience. We can feel this tension when we, like Jonah, know the command to forgive those who hurt us but want to flee and run in the other direction, thinking we can escape God's call. Anger convinces us that we must take matters into our own hands and that we cannot trust God with our circumstances. When we find ourselves running and anger carrying us in the other direction (away from forgiveness, reconciliation, or God), remember that God hates sin because it hurts us and others. He's not punishing us by telling us to forgive and lay down our anger. Instead, by choosing to forgive and release anger, He frees us from the weight of our anger.

Fun fact: *During Jonah's time, the people of Nineveh believed in a divinity who sent messages to them by a person who rose out of the sea as part fish and part man. What better way to be recognized as God's divinely sent messenger to Nineveh than to be thrown up out of the mouth of a great fish, in the presence of witnesses, on the coast of Phoenicia, where the fish-god was a favorite object of worship?*

Managing Anger

Therefore, the question we ask next is how? How do we work through our anger? We can experience freedom from anger by acknowledging our pain and unmet expectations, which is why anger frequently becomes our defense mechanism. Anger is often a protector. It's trying to prevent anyone from getting too close that could possibly hurt us. We work through anger by learning how to express our anger healthily. Below are a few techniques that can help manage anger and biblical practices we are all called to do by God.

One, identify what triggers the anger. How do we respond to most situations that happen? What is the source of anger? We can also find patterns in our lives that cause the most outrage. Identifying what triggers anger is a spiritual discipline where we practice engagement with emotions for self-examination. Self-examination is a discipline (and practice) of reflection aimed at deepening our understanding of ourselves by evaluating our thoughts and actions in light of spiritual principles. This discipline offers a time of reflection to examine our motives, attitudes, and behaviors to recalibrate our hearts toward God. Psalm 139:23-24 reminds us, *"Search me, O God, and know my heart! Try me and know my thoughts! And see if there be any grievous way in me, and lead me in the way everlasting!"*

Two, work to delay the reaction. A way to practically implement this is by counting to ten whenever we feel the sudden rush of emotion come upon us. Our goal is to respond, not react.

Consider a scenario where someone accidentally spills a drink on your laptop. Your immediate emotional reaction might be frustration, anger, or even panic. Reacting impulsively, you might raise your voice, express anger, or blame the person who spilled the drink.

On the other hand, responding involves a more thoughtful and intentional approach. Instead of reacting emotionally, you take a moment to assess the situation, acknowledging your feelings but not letting them control your actions. You might calmly ask the person for assistance cleaning the laptop or, if needed, seek a solution to minimize the damage.

Reacting is often driven by immediate emotions and can lead to impulsive behavior. Responding, however, involves a more measured and intentional approach, considering the broader context and aiming for a constructive resolution. Proverbs 16:32 says, *"Whoever is slow to anger is better than the mighty, and he who rules his spirit than he who takes a city."* This verse describes the difference between reacting and responding. Responding happens by controlling your emotions and choosing a thoughtful course of action.

Control our anger by considering the costs. Consider the side effects of our behavior that can follow our anger. Proverbs 15:18 says, *"A hot-tempered man stirs up strife, but he who is slow to anger quiets contention."* What will the anger we are holding onto cost us? Will it cost us our peace? Our health? Our relationships? Sometimes, we get so focused on seeking revenge that we don't count the cost (and even losses) we experience from the anger we carry.

Surrender our right to retaliate. When we try to get even, we become the epitome of what we hate. Seeking revenge is like drinking poison and expecting the other person to die. This analogy captures the destructive nature of trying to get even. When we engage in a quest for revenge, we often become the embodiment of the qualities we despise in others. It's as if we willingly embrace the negative traits we criticize, thinking it will bring justice or satisfaction.

Think about a scenario where someone wrongs us, and in return, we decide to retaliate with the same hurtful actions. In doing so, we perpetuate a cycle of negativity and mirror the behavior we didn't like in the first place. Ultimately, seeking revenge transforms us into the very thing we stand against while perpetuating a cycle of harm. In our pursuit of revenge, we learn that revenge ultimately harms us more than those we seek to retaliate against. Romans 12:19 reminds us that God will keep His promise, *"Beloved, never avenge yourselves, but leave it to the wrath of God, for it is written, 'Vengeance is mine, I will repay, says the Lord.'"*

Pray and invite God to be near. When anger arises, we don't want the first thing we do to be calling someone to vent and gossip about what happened. We need to give ourselves space to process, pray, and invite God to be near us. He is always with us, but sometimes, we keep him at a distance.

We can pray and process at the same time. We may pray a prayer of supplication, which involves humbly asking God for specific needs, requests, or help. We also may pray a prayer of confession, which involves acknowledging and admitting our sins and shortcomings before God. (This takes humility and recognizing we could also be a part of the problem and the solution.) 1 John 1:9 offers us a simple prayer of confession we can follow, *"If we confess our sins, he is faithful and just to forgive us our sins and to cleanse us from all unrighteousness."* There is also a set of action steps to follow in Philippians 4:6 says, *"Do not be anxious about anything, but in everything by prayer and supplication with thanksgiving, let your requests be made known to God."* These scriptures offer us opportunities to pray and process with the Lord.

Forgiveness can be quite a process to walk through. However, we can forgive even if we are carrying anger. Forgiveness takes place between us and God. We don't need anyone else to forgive. Forgiveness doesn't right wrongs or dismiss their actions, but it releases them from the debt they owe us and puts it in God's hands. It's an intentional decision to cancel the debt owed to us because of an offense.

When we forgive, it can prevent any roots of bitterness from forming. It can control our anger from turning into rage and revenge because we trust God will take care of us. (Even if it doesn't look like we want it to.)

Befriend anger. We spend so much time criticizing ourselves for anything we feel. We hope and wish we could feel something different. Often, we judge ourselves with shame and guilt (not in a way that leads to godly sorrow or repentance) but in a way that produces a cycle of self-hatred. In other words, this cycle produces self-condemnation. Befriending our anger allows us to get curious about it rather than criticize ourselves for experiencing it. How can we "clothe ourselves with compassion and kindness," as Paul describes in Colossians 3:12? Practically speaking, befriending anger allows us to remove judgment and become curious. Then we are free to properly handle and experience our anger to invite Jesus to be near.

Think about feeling frustration and anger due to a challenging situation at work. Instead of suppressing or immediately reacting to the anger, you befriend it. You take a moment to reflect on the source of the anger, possibly recognizing that it stems from feeling undervalued and misunderstood at work (which sometimes leads to a deeper connection or realization of not feeling seen or heard in your life or by people around you when you were a child).

Befriending the anger, you engage in a thoughtful self-examination. Befriending involves asking questions like, "Why does this situation make me feel this way?"

and "What aspect of my values was violated? What expectations do I have that are unmet? Through this process, you can gain insights into personal triggers and underlying issues.

For example, you can begin with constructive action rather than lashing out impulsively or bottling up the anger. Taking action may involve initiating a calm and assertive conversation with colleagues or superiors to address concerns and work toward a resolution. Befriending the anger allows you to use it as a catalyst for positive change rather than allowing it to escalate into destructive behavior.

In this example, befriending anger involves a deliberate and reflective approach, transforming it from an adversary to a companion that provides valuable insights and fuels constructive actions.

These techniques and biblical practices help us navigate through our anger in a way that aligns with God's principles and seeks His heart in the matter. Anger is a God-given emotion that responds to hurt, violation, or a threat. It's not an emotion we have to pretend doesn't exist or that we won't experience it. It's what we do with our anger that determines if we sin. Our anger, when handled with intention, becomes a path to growth, understanding, and, ultimately a closer walk with God.

Further Study Questions

Use the following questions to prompt your study of anger. Study the suggested passages, asking lots of questions to seek understanding. It's hard to change what you aren't willing to confront. Sometimes, the feelings of anger hide a deeper pain the Father wants to heal. He's with you every step of the way.

- How does Matthew 5:21-23 redefine our understanding of anger and its consequences?

    What aspects of God's character do you see in these verses?

    What aspects of humanity do you see in these verses?

    What is Jesus' teaching on anger in this passage?

    How can you live out the truth from this passage?

    What is the source of your anger?

- Discuss the three fundamental beliefs that can trigger anger, as mentioned in the study.

    1.
    2.
    3.

    What are some examples of these beliefs leading to anger in your life?

    1.
    2.
    3.

- According to this study, what is the difference between righteous and fleshly anger?

    Righteous:

    Fleshly:

    What examples can you think of where anger can be considered a mature response to evil?

- How does Jesus differentiate between addressing a person's sinful action and condemning the person concerning anger?

    Addressing:

    Condemning:

    How can we apply this principle in our daily interactions?

- Based on the seven-stage cycle of anger discussed in the study, can you reflect on a time when you've followed this cycle?

    What strategies can you implement to disrupt this cycle and manage your anger effectively? List 3 you will practice:

    Strategy: _____

    I will practice (insert strategy)

    _____

    by (insert how you will practice)

    _____

    on (insert when you will practice or how often)

    _____ .

Strategy: _____

I will practice (insert strategy)

_____

by (insert how you will practice)

_____

on (insert when you will practice or how often)

_____ .

Strategy: _____

I will practice (insert strategy)

_____

by (insert how you will practice)

_____

on (insert when you will practice or how often)

_____ .

- Take time for personal reflection. Are there specific instances, relationships, or circumstances where applying these principles could positively impact your emotional health? List any areas you would like to improve:

    Explore the role of prayer in emotional processing. How can prayer serve as a tool for inviting God into our anger, seeking guidance, and fostering self-awareness? What type of prayer will you experiment with?

    Adoration: Deep love and respect for God, often expressed through worship and praise.

    Breath Prayers: Short, simple prayers spoken in a single breath, allowing for a continuous, meditative conversation with God.

    Confession: Acknowledging and admitting one's sins, mistakes, and shortcomings to God, seeking forgiveness and repentance.

    Consecration: The act of setting oneself apart for sacred purposes, dedicating one's life to God's service and will.

    Guided Prayers: Prayers led by a guide or a specific structure, providing direction and focus during prayer time.

Intercession: Praying on behalf of others, making requests and petitions to God for the well-being and needs of others.

Meditation: Reflective contemplation on a specific scripture, thought, or attribute of God, often seeking deeper understanding and connection with Him.

Petition: Making specific requests or asking God for help, guidance, or intervention in various aspects of life.

Praise: Expressing admiration, reverence, and adoration for God's attributes, deeds, and character.

Praying Scripture: Engaging in prayer using verses or passages from the Bible, aligning one's words with God's Word.

Repentance: Turning away from sin, expressing genuine remorse, and committing to a changed life through God's grace.

Supplication: Earnestly and humbly asking God for specific needs, desires, or help, often involving a sense of urgency.

Thanksgiving: Gratefully acknowledging and expressing appreciation to God for His blessings, provision, and goodness.

Reflect and consider the costs of anger (Proverbs 15:18).

Write out the verse: Proverbs 15:18: _____

_____ _____

_____

_____

_____

_____

_____

In your experience, what are some of the potential side effects or losses associated with unresolved anger?

What is the hardest part for you about trusting God with your feelings of anger? Why?

Describe how you might feel (and live) if you didn't carry anger in your heart.

Notes:

Notes: